A Great Deal!

A Great Deal

Compensation Negotiation for Nurse Practitioners & Physician Assistants

Heidi Bourne, RN

Published by

Open Spaces
P.O. Box 4313, Arcata, CA 95518

This publication is designed to provide accurate and authoritative information about the subject covered. While every precaution has been taken in preparation of this material, the authors assume no liability for damages resulting from the use of the information contained in this publication. The authors are not engaged in rendering legal, accounting, or other professional advice. If legal or other expert advice is required, the services of an appropriate professional should be sought. Please note, some of the stories in this publication are true. All names have been changed to fictional characters to illustrate the examples. The authors assume no liability for damages resulting from the use of these names. For simplicity throughout this book, the employer is referred to in the male gender.

ISBN 0-9654977-4-7

Contributing Editors: Carol Sweig, Rebecca Bender
Cover Design and Book Production: Creative Type, Arcata, CA
Book Design: Bonnie Fisk-Hayden, Point Reyes Station, CA

Printed in the United States of America

Fourth Edition

Foreword

As a society, we are taught to live and work by the rules, and not to question authority too much. We are certainly not taught to negotiate. Going to bat for ourselves in the context of a negotiation is often unknown territory. There is an unspoken, unwritten expectation that we as healthcare professionals must be *unconditional* caregivers. This is particularly true for women, and especially true for nurses. While this phenomenon in no way excludes men, it is less pervasive in male dominated professions. No one can give unconditionally or within unacceptable parameters for very long. This perception on the part of our patients, our employers, and our neighbors ultimately undermines the quality of our work and our self-worth.

Defining values and standing behind them is what ***A Great Deal*** is all about. Making sure that the terms of your job meet your needs honors you by recognizing your hard-earned skills and talents. Laying the foundation for your work life is entirely up to you.

As a nurse who consistently stirred the pot at work by saying what I thought, and not always to the right person, it became clear that the only way to change an unacceptable situation was to take some risks. I frequently sought out my colleagues and superiors with ideas for this or that, and I was undeterred when my ideas were rejected. I adjusted and tried again. Ultimately I founded Western Practitioner Resources, a leading placement service for nurse practitioners and physician assistants. ***A Great Deal*** is a result of spending many years helping to design and negotiate compensation packages, and encouraging my colleagues to speak out.

Heidi Bourne

TABLE OF CONTENTS

Introduction

PART I

Benefits

PART II

Negotiation Planner

PART III

PART IV

Introduction: A Great Deal

Preparing for Compensation Negotiation

PREPARING FOR COMPENSATION NEGOTIATION

"A Great Deal" is a working guide. It is loaded with information and tools to help you prepare for an upcoming compensation negotiation and overall employment agreement. Use these ideas to create a real working agreement with your employer.

A Great Deal assumes you are being offered a new job or wish to renegotiate your present compensation. You probably already know something about what to expect in salary and other benefits. This guide suggests many options for securing what you need *before* you begin work. The more you know about your employer in general, and their policies in particular before you enter a negotiation, the more prepared you will be.

PART I of **A Great Deal** is a discussion of the various elements of a typical compensation package. Each discussion concludes with a section, *Negotiation Strategy*, which suggests ways to get what you need.

PART II is the *Negotiation Planner*, which takes you through the process of writing your own employment contract.

PART III is a discussion of the *Contractual Agreement* and offers several *Sample Agreements* which address full time and part time jobs, as well as those working as independent contractors.

PART IV provides detailed and specific information about *Resumes* and *Cover Letters*, with samples of each, as well as a discussion about the *Interview Process*.

A Great Deal concludes with several blank pages for *Notes*, a convenient place to write down your ideas as you go. Use this guide to focus your thoughts. It will prepare you to confidently and successfully negotiate with your employer, your negotiating partner.

Your Power to Negotiate

Never assume that your compensation package is already decided. Whether you are starting a new job or thinking about how to improve your current situation, you can make a significant difference by asking for what you need. Some employers, especially large ones, will have fairly rigid guidelines; others will be more flexible. Even the toughest, most set-in-his-ways employer wants you to feel fairly treated. It is true that some employers are fundamentally unreasonable and inflexible. These are the most difficult to negotiate with and sometimes to work with. But even these employers want you to look forward to coming to work. Your employer will have ideas about what he wants and why. He, too, must make those positions clear. Until everyone's needs are known, the outcome of any negotiation is unpredictable. Don't underestimate your ability to influence the negotiation process, especially the end result.

Prepare for the Process

Before you enter the negotiation process, decide what you want, and why you want it. Having your ducks in a row allows you to present your needs with clarity, confidence, and objectivity. Be sure you understand all of the elements of compensation. If you have a question, don't be reluctant to ask your future employer for clarification. *Make him your ally*. Do not consult with existing staff unless the employer offers you the option. (Refer to *A WORD ABOUT CONFIDENTIALITY* on page 14) Remember, money is just one part of how you will be paid for your efforts. This guide will help you decide what's reasonable.

Timing Is Crucial

Be absolutely certain your negotiation conference happens when you and your employer are not tired. Avoid the end of the day. Avoid Fridays. If you are a new employee, have the conference before you begin work. *You are the most powerful before you work the first day*. Remember, you've been hired because you are wanted. Your new employer believes you are valuable. If you are renegotiating as a veteran employee, decide when and where you will find your employer the most relaxed. Make an appointment. You want his undivided attention.

Listen Well

Too often, people go into a negotiation conference with so much attention on what they have to say that they do not listen well. If you really listen, you learn more, and your negotiation will have a better outcome. Don't back yourself into a corner with preconceptions or false assumptions. In fact, make no assumptions at all. When your employer offers something that doesn't fit with your expectations, tell him that and say why. Stay neutral. If you don't understand the reasons for his positions, say so. Ask for more explanation. Do not take anything personally. A fair-minded negotiating partner will learn from his own explanations. Ideally, both you and your employer will be articulate, intelligent, unselfish, and objective. Use this technique to get yourself ***A Great Deal!***

Win Win

Most negotiations take several meetings to reach a conclusion. Take your time making your decisions. Your employer, your negotiating partner, will expect nothing less. You owe it to yourself to make sure your legitimate needs are met. You must decide what that means. You owe it to your employer to give as much as you get. If you and your employer traded places, your perspectives would change and be significantly enhanced. Most compensation negotiations conclude with something unexpected. (Refer to *CONTINUING EDUCATION* on page 31)

Put It In Writing

No matter what, put your agreement in writing. Written agreements carry great weight. Most employers will expect to do the writing, but almost no one likes doing the work. A smart alternative is to offer to write your employer a draft letter stating your understanding of the agreement you've made. When you do the writing, it gets done promptly, and you save your employer the chore. You protect your confidentiality, you include everything you believe to be contained in the agreement, and you discourage the employer from re-thinking and re-opening the negotiation. Of course, he may make corrections if he thinks you've erred or omitted something. Once you've agreed that the letter is an accurate statement of your agreement, write it up. Both you and your employer sign it and keep a copy.

The Last Word

The best negotiations end with no one having the last word. Rather, agreements are reached which are fair and help to insure an honorable and respectful working relationship. What a great deal!

A WORD ABOUT CONFIDENTIALITY: Most employers prefer that a compensation package be kept private to avoid comparisons among employees. Confidentiality benefits you, bolsters the respect between you and your employer, and enlarges your negotiating options. The benefits and importance of this cannot be overstated. Here's a true story.

> *Julian found a job he really wanted. The employer was eager to hire him as his skills and personality fit the needs of the health center. Julian came to the job with a couple of years experience and was fairly confident in his skills. While interviewing, he met several of the other providers who clearly liked their jobs. When Julian was formally offered the job and given the details of the compensation package, he phoned one of the PA's he'd met to compare the offer with the compensation of this PA. Julian wanted to be sure his offer was competitive. The staff PA told Julian that he should never accept such an offer, as it was nothing like his. Now Julian was stuck. He wanted the job, the offer met his needs, but he knew his new colleague was earning more money.*
>
> *Next, the staff PA went to the employer to report his conversation with Julian and asked the employer to increase the salary in the offer. As a result, the employer lost trust and respect for both Julian and the staff PA, and nearly rescinded Julian's offer entirely. In the end, Julian did get the job, but with the terms of the original offer. Later negotiations were much more difficult, and it took the employer a long time to fully trust both Julian and the staff PA.*

PART I

Compensation

Money in your Pocket: Compensation in Dollars

Money in your Name: Compensation in Deferred Dollars

SALARY

Fee-for-Service vs. Managed Care

Fee-for-service practices are those that are reimbursed by private insurance companies as services are provided. The managed care company, the HMO, funds practices by assigning a given number of patients to the practice, "covered lives", for which they pay the practice a set fee per patient per month. This is capitation.

Not so long ago, an experienced practitioner could often write his own ticket within acceptable parameters, as fee-for-service based practices could afford to pay practitioners on productivity alone. Now, only the most profitable private practices offer compensation using productivity as a significant factor in determining the overall wage. The transition to managed care in many parts of the country has made this method of compensation unaffordable and uncommon. While productivity remains a critical factor in both managed care and fee-for-service practices, capitation determines the budget and the individual NP or PA can do little to increase the revenue based on patient visits alone.

Managed care has caused a definite shift downward in salaries for NP's, PA's, and MD's. It has created a very real competitive atmosphere among these providers, and sometimes for the same jobs. As such, NP's and PA's must adjust their expectations.

The "Going Rate"

Salaries are usually determined by the "going rate" for your kind of services in your geographical area. In general, salaries are based on geography, experience, the nature of the practice, the total compensation package, and the idiosyncrasies of the employer. Certain prosperous practices are able to pay higher salaries. The real differences in salaries are typically accounted for by the supply and demand in a particular area or specialty. As in every other job, your salary really depends on why you are needed, and what you bring with you: your training, experience, special talents (like Spanish fluency), enthusiasm, flexibility, or some other intangible.

Shooting For The Moon.... Or.... Shooting Yourself In The Foot

We all want to earn as much money as we can, and there is nothing wrong with aiming high. The trick is to know when to stop. Once you've reached common ground, refrain from going back for more. It can backfire. There is a tendency to believe that if the negotiation was easy, you didn't ask for enough. Not true. In all likelihood, the negotiation was easy because you and your employer were reasonable. You want your employer in your court. As with any job, you will be expected to prove yourself. Keeping something in your back pocket for future negotiations is smart. This underscores the importance of knowing what you need before you begin to negotiate.

The Real Numbers

Nationwide, annual salaries can range from $40,000 to $80,000 for full time work. Hourly, that means $19 to $40 for a practitioner working in primary care. Practitioners in some specialties earn as much as $95,000, while many working in inner city or rural clinics earn substantially less than the norm. Breaking this down further, the most common hourly range is $24 - S35. New graduates can expect to earn $24 - $28 per hour to start, $49,920 to $58,240 annually, while experienced providers expect to earn more.

Determining the appropriate salary or hourly wage for a part time position can be tricky. It depends on how part time the job actually is. Sometimes these jobs offer prorated benefits, sometimes they offer full benefits, and some offer no benefits at all. (The *Negotiation Planner* later on in this guide illustrates the formula for determining salaries in further detail.)

Warning: Some employers prefer to pay practitioners by the hour. In general, this is not a good idea in full time positions, as such arrangements encourage clock watching and tend to limit other important benefits that are common with salaried positions.* There is a notable exception. Practitioners working in emergency medicine and urgent care are almost always paid by the hour, as are the physicians with whom they work.

Temporary work, *locum tenens*, has a different set of parameters. Jobs that do not offer benefits almost always pay higher hourly wages than those with benefits. Practitioners working in temporary jobs commonly earn $30 to $35 per hour, sometimes as high as $45 per hour, though this is rare.

If you choose to work in a temporary capacity, or as an independent contractor, be sure you understand how the IRS addresses this kind of income, as well as how the IRS defines "independent contractor." A defining factor of an independent contractor is a person who does not work at any given site a majority of his time. As an independent contractor or temporary provider, you will likely be paid your wage without any payroll taxes being withheld, and the IRS expects you to report this income. In addition, the employer is required to report all compensation paid in excess of $600 per year to all persons providing this kind of service. The IRS routinely verifies the legitimacy of wages paid to independent contractors and temporary providers.

* Be sure you know what the laws in your state are pertaining to overtime. Overtime is almost never paid with salaried positions. However, NP's and PA's whose wages are paid hourly are often exempt from receiving overtime because the profession commands wages in excess of two times minimum wage. Check your state laws.

Resources

There are clearly a large number of variables that influence salary ranges and the going rate on a regular basis. Additional information is available from the American Academy of Physician Assistants (AAPA), the American College of Nurse Practitioners (ACNP), the American Academy of Nurse Practitioners, and Nurse Practitioner Support Services (NPSS). The AAPA and NPSS do excellent and thorough salary surveys, and the ACNP and AANP have excellent information available on many different issues.

American Academy of
Physician Assistants (AAPA)
950 N. Washington Street
Arlington, VA 22314-1552
(703) 836-2272
http://www.aapa.org

American College of
Nurse Practitioners (ACNP)
503 Capitol Ct. NE #300
Washington, DC 20002
(202) 546-4825
http://www.nurse.org

American Academy of
Nurse Practitioners
P.O. Box 12846
Austin, TX 78711
(512) 442-4262
http://www.aanp.org

Nurse Practitioner
Support Services
10024 S.E. 240th St., Suite #102
Kent, WA 98031
(253) 852-9042
http://www.nurse.net/

NEGOTIATION STRATEGY

You have every right to expect enough money. That means an amount reasonably close to what others with your qualifications and experience are earning in your area. Do not make the mistake of asking for a specific amount initially. Rather, ask the employer what salary he expects to pay. Let him know you understand your salary is tied to his ability to pay and to the rest of your compensation package. If he suggests an amount considerably under your expectations, tell him why you are surprised. If he is reasonably close to what you expected, consider his offer seriously. The game of start high/offer low is unproductive and wastes time. Say what you need. Be sure to factor in the rest of your compensation package, as it will certainly influence the dollar amount you require. The Negotiation Planner *will guide you through the process of determining how salary relates to the package as a whole.*

Bonus & Incentive Plans

The Bonus

Bonuses often come as a pleasant surprise, usually when the practice has done well and the employer wishes to recognize the significant contributions of the practitioner with dollars. Keep in mind, however, a bonus is not salary. It adds to the employer's overhead, so he must feel you're worth what you're getting. You pay tax on extra dollars received, and your employer will be required to withhold and pay appropriate payroll tax, as well.

Bonuses are paid for two reasons: you earn them or your employer chooses to "share the wealth". Some bonuses are prearranged based on the achievement of goals. If these goals are not specific, hard feelings often result when an employee's expectations are not met. Again, make no assumptions. Without mutual understanding and a written agreement, you may be left with no concrete way to object if the bonus is withheld.

The Incentive

While there is no negotiation for a surprise bonus, you may negotiate for additional monetary rewards for your performance. For example, if you work quickly, you might ask for additional money for seeing more than a given number of patients in an allotted time. Or you might ask to receive extra compensation when patients with a choice repeatedly request an appointment with you. Commonly, incentives range between 3% and 10% of gross collections on your patients. Both the high and low ends of that range are unusual. This kind of incentive pay should be part of your regular payroll check, usually paid two to three months after the fact to allow for collections. Your employer cannot be expected to pay incentive dollars out before he has them in hand. Again, any incentive plan needs to be put in writing. It benefits everyone.

NEGOTIATION STRATEGY

Keep any bonus or incentive request in your back pocket. Go through the entire compensation package with your employer before mentioning a bonus or incentive. If he brings it up earlier in the conversation, just ask what he expects to do. Do not comment thereafter until the rest of the compensation is settled or almost settled. Then you will be in a position to propose a bonus or incentive based on a variety of factors: acquiring new and valuable skills, your excellent performance, or adding something valuable to the practice that doesn't exist without you. Deciding what to propose and when to propose it will depend on everything that has gone before in the negotiation. It will also depend on your best guess as to what is fair and what you are likely to get. Never ask for a bonus or incentive when you've already got a great compensation package. But, when you feel you've compromised in key areas and the balance is not quite even, use these elements as possible equalizers. Again, the purpose is to create and maintain a healthy working relationship, while paying you appropriately for your work. Remember, take your time. Most negotiations take several conversations to reach agreement.

Retirement Plans

There are many different kinds of retirement plans. Most plans are structured according to specific guidelines dictated by the Internal Revenue Service. "Retirement" implies that dollars received by you are tax deferred. If our tax laws remain close to what they have been for many years, you will be encouraged by the federal government to save for your retirement. It is smart to take full advantage of any retirement plan offered. Tax-free dollars saved and invested wisely are a wonderful asset.

Some employers will offer to contribute to your retirement, like your own IRA. Your employer may offer a plan wherein he matches your own contribution. Some plans require the employer to invest for you based on a fixed formula as he invests for himself. As a participant, you are entitled to a complete, written explanation of any retirement plan offered. Take the time to read and understand it. The time spent is absolutely worth it. You must make sure you know if and how the retirement plan affects your actual take home pay. The more you know, the more you can plan. If you work with an accountant or other tax advisor, it is worth the fee to discuss how any retirement plan affects your tax payments and planning.

NEGOTIATION STRATEGY

Many retirement plans are not optional, so there is nothing to negotiate. The IRS requires 100% participation by all employees who meet specific criteria, typically length of employment, depending on the plan. It is likely that your employer will see his contribution to your retirement as a benefit to you, and it is. In some cases, it is also an important benefit to him, allowing him to maximize the contribution to his own retirement.

Other less formal plans allow you to choose not to participate. That choice is a negotiating chip and should be put on the table only after you have a thorough understanding of what you are not getting. Here's an example. The employer offers to contribute $100 per month to your IRA when his profits exceed 10% in any month. How are his profits calculated? Odds are good he will not allow you to audit his books every month. His contribution to your IRA remains entirely optional. As an alternative, ask for a flat amount contributed to your IRA annually, regardless of your employer's profits. Five percent of your gross earnings is not unheard of. Or, you may wish to negotiate for a benefit other than a retirement plan. Know what you need from this job, and consider retirement as a part of your entire compensation package.

Benefits

Time Off

Insurance

Continuing Education

The Bottom Line

Time Off

Vacation

Two weeks paid vacation in the first year is customary for full time work. In part time jobs, paid time off is typically prorated according to the full time equivalent, "FTE". Most employers will ask that you work six months without vacation, whether your position is part or full time. This gives you adequate time to settle in, and be well on the way to establishing your place in the practice. Staff, patients, and your employer need time to get to know you. The amount of paid vacation commonly increases along with the number of years of employment. However, few employers will give more than four weeks paid vacation, as extended absences are costly and significantly compromise your practice. Be sure you know the specific details of your employer's vacation policy before you begin work.

Holidays

You can expect six to twelve paid holidays per year. Many employers close their offices on legal holidays. They specify which those will be and pay you when the office is closed. Here you will be bound by the office policy. In some specialties, legal holidays are treated as normal days: urgent care, emergency medicine, and surgical specialties are examples. Depending on your state laws, you may or may not receive special pay for working those days. Make sure you know your employer's policies.

Sick Leave

Here there is great variation among employers. Some have no formal policy, expecting you will be out occasionally and relying on your sense of responsibility to come to work if you can. Others will offer between one half and one full paid day off each month. Some will pay you for unused sick days at the end of the year. Fairness demands that your illness not penalize your employer.

NEGOTIATION STRATEGY

Remember, you have a lot of power before you work your first day. If you have plans to be away before you are entitled to paid vacation, negotiate that before you start work. Most employers are flexible, if you make advance arrangements. If the vacation policy of your employer provides less paid time away than you believe you need, tell him that with your reasons. For example, he may be willing to negotiate unpaid time off or more paid time taken in long weekends. You might ask for a regular half day off each week or every other week, or you may ask for a schedule that accommodates your child's school or summer routine. Many practices have a slower time when your absence would be less important to the smooth running of the business, or even beneficial.

The options for time off are many. Be sure you get what you need. If you really require a half-day off every week, go to bat for yourself to get it. Be willing to compromise, even sacrifice in some other area. Keep in mind that you are working to satisfy both your own and your employer's needs. When you are away, the needs of the practice continue to exist, especially when you're good at your work. Your employer wants you at work, but he understands your need to breathe. He needs to breathe, too.

INSURANCE

Malpractice, Health, Life & Disability

Many employers treat insurance as an expense to the business and expect to pay all costs. Others see their role as the vehicle through which you can buy insurance at a lower rate than would be available to you on an individual basis. Some form of insurance is almost always available to you through your employer.

Malpractice Insurance

It is customary that most employers provide you with full malpractice liability coverage at no cost to you. However, carrying your own independent policy not only increases your protection, but it elevates your level of professionalism, increases your job options, and makes you more powerful. This is especially valuable for PA's and NP's who consistently work in a *locum tenens* capacity. It allows the practitioner to begin work immediately instead of waiting for clearance from the employer's carrier.

Insurance companies commonly offer coverage ranging from $1 million per claim with a total of $3 million in claims per year per practitioner, to $5 million per claim and a total of $5 million per year per practitioner. Annual premiums for a $1 million/$3 million policy typically cost about $800 for full time FNP's, and as much as $2,000 for PA's. The rates are commonly the same for both employees and independent contractors.

Coverage is called "Claims Made" or "Occurrence". A "Claims Made" policy covers you for any claim made against you as long as the policy is active and you are listed as an insured party. You must be currently working with the specific employer holding the policy. A "Claims Made" policy does *not* provide "tail" coverage. Tail coverage provides for you after you leave the practice and/or after the practice ceases to exist. An "Occurrence" policy covers you for all claims made against you regardless of your employment, as it includes tail coverage. It is absolutely essential that you understand what you are getting.

When your employer does provide your coverage, it does not mean you automatically have adequate coverage. Ask to see a copy of the policy. It is tedious reading and worth the time. You must make sure you are adequately protected. It is not difficult to imagine being sued by a disgruntled patient for a perceived failure on your part long after you've changed jobs. Under the coverage your employer provides, would the insurance company pay the costs if your were found to have been negligent? If there is not satisfactory tail coverage as a part of your policy, you must decide to either take the risk or buy additional insurance on your own. Both options can be expensive.

Nationwide, there are a number of companies who provide individual malpractice policies to nurse practitioners and physician assistants independently. Some are listed below. In addition, malpractice policies may be available through AAPA, ACNP, or your state NP or PA organization.

Seabury & Smith
332 So. Michigan Ave
Chicago, IL 60604
(800) 621-3008

National Professional Group
875 N. Michigan Ave, 21st Floor
Chicago, IL 60611
(800) 253-5486

Healthcare Providers
Service Organization
159 East County Line Rd
Hatboro, PA 19040-1218
(800) 982-9491

Wood Insurance Group
1430 E. Missouri Ave, Suite 225
Phoenix, AZ 85014
(800) 695-0219

Health Insurance

Nothing is as complicated as health insurance. Every employer must choose whether or not to offer health insurance. In paying for coverage, the employer takes on a significant expense, as well as a complex set of additional decisions. He must decide which insurer to trust. How much insurance is enough? The employer must consider the inevitable increases in premium costs. Can employees be asked to pay some part of the cost? While employer paid health insurance is often part of a benefit package, you may be required to work a given number of months before you are eligible to participate.

The cost of health care is so great, no one can really afford to be without some form of insurance. If your employer does not provide it, and you are not covered by your spouse's policy, it is wise to ask for additional compensation to help defray the cost of buying insurance on your own.

Life Insurance

Life insurance is frequently offered as part of some other benefit. Group plans can offer individuals up to $50,000 in term life insurance. Some retirement plans and some health insurance plans include a life insurance provision. Ask about it. It is rare that an employer will offer life insurance unless it is a part of something else.

Disability Insurance

In many states, employers are required to withhold a very small percentage from your gross wages and deposit this money into the State Disability Insurance Fund. If you become temporarily or permanently disabled, you can make a claim with your local Employment Development Department. How much money you receive and for how long is determined by how much you have worked over the previous 18 months, and how much money you earned. In most cases, additional disability insurance coverage is not provided by the employer, but there may be an option through your employer to purchase an independent policy. Don't hesitate to ask.

NEGOTIATION STRATEGY

Decide what is important to you. Know why, for example, you must have that low deductible medical coverage. Know why you need or can do without tail coverage. Bring these issues to the attention of your employer at a moment in the negotiations when you've already established your credibility as a reasonable person. Protect your interests, and bear in mind the employer's costs and concerns.

Continuing Education - CE

Continuing Education requirements vary from state to state and from profession to profession. It is your responsibility to know just what is required of you. It is fair to expect your employer to give you three to five days paid time off per year to obtain the necessary hours. Generally, employers are accustomed to paying a stipend for this purpose, and it is reasonable to expect between $500 and $2000. As you consider your CE needs, keep in mind that your continued education benefits you, your employer, and your patients by maintaining and expanding your current skills and knowledge. This enhances your value in the practice. The *Negotiation Planner* offers some ideas for approaching and itemizing Continuing Education requirements. Another story:

Sarah, a nurse practitioner with one year of internal medicine experience, met with her employer to renegotiate her compensation package. Over the previous year, she became involved in a diabetes research program as part of her regular job. She began to spend more and more time with the patients involved in the program, and discovered how much she enjoyed research. There were several opportunities coming up in the next year to attend diabetes education conferences that would significantly enhance her knowledge of the disease and her effectiveness as a practitioner and researcher.

Sarah's current CE benefit allowed for five days paid time off at $30 per hour, $1,200, and $800 for tuition. She wanted ten days paid time off and $1,500 for tuition to attend the upcoming conferences. In concrete numbers, she was requesting an additional $1,900, totaling $3,900 in CE expense for the year. Sarah's employer saw the wisdom and direct benefit to him in sending Sarah to the meetings, but couldn't afford the increase without adjusting some other part of her compensation package.

Sarah got creative. She wrote a grant to the local Diabetes Foundation asking them to fund one half of her educational expenses for that year. She then went back to her employer and asked him to match whatever amount she raised from the Diabetes Foundation. Sarah's employer was delighted with the solution, and thoroughly impressed with her determination and creativity. He not only matched the grant, but also gave her an unexpected increase in salary.

NEGOTIATION STRATEGY

The CE stipend is a great bargaining chip. It is fair to assume you will receive at least $500, so if something else is more important to you, be willing to forego the stipend entirely. For example, you may want an extra Friday off to allow for a long weekend's vacation. Is that worth $500? You decide. In general, do not ask for reimbursement for travel, meals, hotel, etc. Rather, try to get your CE tuition paid by your employer, accept the offered stipend, or settle for just the paid time off. Again, you want to go away from the negotiation feeling fairly treated. Give your negotiating partner good reasons to do what you want him to do.

The Bottom Line

No two jobs are alike, as most professionals know. Most of us have experienced good ones and not such good ones, and the reasons for those differences are many. Think of your total compensation package as one element of your job, your professional practice. You may value a lower paying job because it's walking distance between your home and your kids' school. A higher paying job requiring a grueling commute may be impossible. Maybe you really want to work in a special practice and can sacrifice something else. Sometimes practitioners love their jobs because they love their patients, and nothing else matters.

Every workplace has special circumstances that deeply influence feelings of joy and loyalty or negativity and dissatisfaction. Whether or not you receive a particular benefit, whether you receive a specific amount of money...what matters is the whole deal. Sometimes it takes leaving one job for another to realize what we had before. Try to keep the big picture in mind. For any job to be truly satisfying, you must look forward to going to work most days. When you start dreading it or resenting it, you owe it to yourself to fix it or change it.

The power to change comes from knowledge and convictions. Know what you want and why you want it. Be confident that you *can* get what you need. Use the *Negotiation Planner* to create your own **Great Deal!**

Never forget your power to influence and positively improve your own working life. Using that power will take work and courage, and the dividends are enormous.

Part II

Negotiation Planner

Worksheets

NEGOTIATION PLANNER

This *Negotiation Planner* is designed to guide your thinking through your compensation package. Keep in mind that a full package includes much more than salary. As you fill in the blanks, refer back to the appropriate sections of ***A Great Deal***. Use the information to help you decide what you want, what you need, and what you will take to the conversation with your employer. Try not to skip filling in any part of the *Negotiation Planner*. Putting your information, hopes, and good ideas in writing will give you focus and power. Also, writing it all out will force you to really think about your job as a whole. You may wish to make a copy of the *Planner* before you begin to fill it out. Working your way through it may result in surprising changes as you go along.

POSITION
Job Description, Support, & Schedule

Job Description: Include your scope of practice based on your level of skills and experience.

____

____

____

____

____

Support: Will you work with other providers? How much autonomy will you have? Who is your immediate backup or supervising physician, and who is the backup when he is unavailable? How will you work with the office staff?

____

____

____

Schedule: Current, Proposed, and Ideal

Outline a typical week's schedule as it is currently, include any call, and the total numbers of hours scheduled:

____

____

____

____

Your ideal schedule:

____

____

____

____

Proposed Schedule:

____

____

____

____

Will this schedule change on a regular basis? If so, how?

____

____

____

____

How does your proposed schedule compare to the practice's business hours as a whole?

____

____

____

____

____

____

Where can you compromise?

____

____

____

____

____

____

____

Create an acceptable alternative:

____

____

____

____

____

____

____

COMPENSATION
Salary, Bonus, & Incentive

SALARY: It is not unusual for employers to offer an hourly rate and then pay it as an annual salary. Here is a conversion formula.

FULL TIME 40 hours per week x 52 weeks per year = 2080 hours per year
wage per hour x 2080 hours = annual salary

EXAMPLE $28 per hour x 2080 hours = $58,240 annual salary

There are two ways to calculate a part time salary:

HALF TIME 20 hours per week x 52 weeks per year = 1040 hours per year

$28 per hour x 1040 hours = $29,120 annual salary
or
$58,240 x 50% = $29,120

EXAMPLES
5 days per week = 100% = $58, 240
4 days per week = 80% = $46, 592
3 days per week = 60% = $34, 944

OFFERED SALARY ______________

GOING RATE ______________

If you do not know what your employer will offer, fill in this blank with the "going rate" for providers doing your kind of work in your geographical area. Wait to fill out the minimum acceptable salary until you've worked through the rest of the *Negotiation Planner*. You may well change your mind about that bottom line number several times.

DESIRED SALARY ____

MINIMUM ACCEPTABLE __________________________________

____

FREQUENCY OF PAYMENT AND PAYMENT DATES

____

____

____

BONUS: You have no control over when you get a bonus, so there is nothing to negotiate. Sometimes a bonus takes the form of an early, unscheduled salary increase, or sometimes it is given in a lump sum of money to thank you for a job well done. However, you and your employer may propose a bonus agreement to be paid when you achieve specific goals.

Goals ____

____

____

____

By When? ____

____

Your Benefit ____

____

____

Your Employer's Benefit ___________________________________

____

____

Offered Bonus ____

____

Your Proposed Bonus ________________________________

____

INCENTIVE: If you know your employer's incentive policy, fill in the blank. Otherwise, fill in the space provided for you to construct what you believe would be an appropriate incentive provision. The blank labeled "Basis" should be completed with information about how the incentive is calculated and justified. If you decide to propose an incentive, you will need a good, well argued basis for your proposal. Give particular attention to when incentive dollars are paid. This can be a great bargaining chip.

Offered Incentive________________ **Payment Dates** ______________

Basis ____

____

Proposed Incentive________________ **Payment Dates** ______________

Basis ____

____

Retirement Plans

Describe any retirement plan you already have. Those who are married are frequently co-beneficiaries of their spouse's retirement system. Find out what you can about your employer's retirement plans and how they are funded.

Your own retirement plan(s) ____________________________

____

____

Your Contributions ______________________________

____

____

Your $ Benefit ______________________________

____

____

Employer's Retirement Plan(s) ______________________________

____

____

Employer's Contribution ______________________________

____

____

Your Contribution (if any) ______________________________

____

Your $ Benefit ______________________________

____

Time Off
Vacation, Holidays, & Sick Leave

Find out as much as possible about your employer's policies for paid time off. Ask about any restrictions, including how long you must work before becoming eligible for vacation. Is there an increasing vacation scale based on your longevity in the job? An employer may offer three weeks vacation after two years with only two weeks allowed to be taken consecutively. Another may require that all staff vacations be evenly spread over the entire year to prevent large seasonal gaps. The allocation of specific vacation dates will normally be based on seniority. Decide how you would structure your time off to perfectly fit your needs. Then think about how you might compromise. Keep in mind that many things are negotiable and fairness carries great weight.

Offered Paid Vacation ______________________________

Restrictions ______________________________

Paid Holidays ______________________________

____

Sick Leave (paid and unpaid) ______________________________

YOUR PREFERENCES

Vacation ______________________________

Sick Leave ______________________________

Other Personal Days (include reason) ______________________________

____

____

____

____

Insurance
Malpractice, Health, Life, & Disability

MALPRACTICE INSURANCE: provided by your employer

Carrier ____________________

____

Type ("Claims Made" or "Occurrence") ____________________

____

Amount of Coverage ____________________

____

Additional malpractice insurance you may wish to purchase: an occurance policy which includes tail coverage, or tail coverage alone.

Carrier ____________________

Amount of Coverage ____________________

Policy Cost ____________________

HEALTH INSURANCE: Describe the health insurance coverage offered by your employer. Include any non-optional cost to you like deductibles or co-payments. Find out if the policy covers your spouse and dependents or just yourself. This information should be readily available, as most employees will have identical or very similar coverage. Some employers will offer choices. You may decide to decline the offer of health insurance and seek coverage independently or through your spouse's plan. Make careful comparisons of all benefits to get the most for your money.

Employer's Plan and Carrier ____________________

Family Members Covered ______________________________

____

Cost to You ______________________________

Alternative Employer Plan(s) ______________________________

____

Family Members Covered ______________________________

Cost to You ______________________________

Individual Non-Employer Plan ______________________________

____

Cost to You ______________________________

Spouse's Plan ______________________________

Cost to You ______________________________

LIFE INSURANCE & DISABILITY INSURANCE

Before you enter the negotiation, find out if your employer offers any life or disability insurance. It is unusual for these policies to be offered; however, it may be possible for your employer to assist you in obtaining this coverage economically. Ask him about it. If you have other insurance coverage of this nature, note it here. Remember to include any disability insurance provided by your state and for which your employer automatically withholds from your wages.

EMPLOYER COVERAGE – Life

Carrier ______________________________

Type ("Term" or "Whole Life") ______________________________

Amount of Coverage ______________________________

____

EMPLOYER COVERAGE - Disability

Carrier ______________________________

Amount of Coverage ______________________________

When do payments begin? ______________________________

How long do they continue? ______________________________

OTHER COVERAGE (independent purchased)

Life Insurance (Carrier) ______________________________

Type ("Term" or "Whole Life") ______________________________

Amount of Coverage and Cost: ______________________________

Disability Insurance (State or Private Carrier) ______________________________

Amount of Coverage ______________________________

____

When Payments Begin and Cost ______________________________

How long to do they continue? ______________________________

Continuing Education - CE

Continuing Education costs vary enormously, depending on location and many other factors. If you are a new graduate, find out how much CE hours generally cost. If you are an experienced practitioner, try to come up with your own average cost per hour of CE. If you expect to travel away from your area for CE, be sure to factor into your average the cost of transportation, hotels, food, etc. Continuing Education is an unavoidable expense. You must decide how to cover it.

State Required CE ____________________

ESTIMATED CE COSTS PER YEAR

Tuition ____________________

Transportation ____________________

Lodging & Food ____________________

Cost per Hour of CE or Average Cost per Course ____________

TOTAL ESTIMATED COSTS PER YEAR ____________

EMPLOYER CONTRIBUTION

Any Employer Required CE ____________________

Paid Time Off ____________________

Unpaid Time Off ____________________

Expense Stipend ____________________

TOTAL COST PER YEAR ____________

EMPLOYER CONTRIBUTION ____________

YOUR COST ____________

The Bottom Line

This is a very important element in the *Negotiation Planner*. There are reasons you want this job, and reasons your employer wants you. List them all.

Why you want this job

____

____

____

____

____

____

____

____

Why your employer wants you

____

____

____

____

____

____

____

____

In Conclusion

Now you are ready to take everything you've just written and put in into a formal proposal. Use the format of the *Sample Agreements* that follow as a guide. Before you do this, it's a good idea to go back and re-read everything you've just written and take some time to just think about it. You might come up with some new ideas.

What are the elements in your proposal that are especially important to you? What is especially important to your employer? *Be prepared to compromise*. By remembering why you want this job and why your employer wants you, you can find the confidence to ask for what you need.

The information and tools provided in this guide are not a magic bullet. Some will work beautifully, some will not. Negotiating your own compensation package may not be easy, but it can be very rewarding. It requires creativity, patience, clear thinking, taking some risks, lots of courage, and most importantly the willingness to go through the process. Most negotiations have their difficult moments, and everyone is bound to learn a lot. In the end, negotiating gives you control of your work life, promotes balance, enhances your relationships, prevents needless suffering, and it just might get you a little closer to your perfect job.

Part III
The Written Contract

Contractual Agreement

Sample Agreements

Contractual Agreement

It is exceedingly important that you have a written contractual agreement with your employer. This insures that both of you have clear expectations about your job and how you will be compensated. It cannot be written until the conclusion of your negotiations, when you and your employer have reached agreement. Remember to be the one to put it in writing.

The contractual agreement describes various details including salary and benefit increases, frequency of performance evaluations, any probationary period, the manner in which your agreement renews itself, and how either party can terminate the relationship. Here is an example.

> The probationary period will be for the first 90 days of employment. During which time either the practitioner or employer may withdraw from this agreement with one day's notice. Thereafter, both parties agree to give 30 days written notice of such withdrawal. The employer can give one month's salary in lieu of one month's written notice to withdraw from this contract.
>
> Performance evaluations will be given at the end of the probationary period and every six months thereafter, or when either party requests one. Salary and benefits will be evaluated every 12 months, and increases will be given on the basis of cost of living adjustment or merit.* This agreement automatically renews itself on a monthly basis until either party gives one month's notice to terminate employment.

The point of the example is to underscore the importance of obtaining absolute clarity and agreement and then writing it down. Here's a true story.

Alex was an unemployed physician assistant accustomed to earning $72,000 per year with full benefits. He had many years' experience in family practice and women's health and was having some difficulty finding the right job. As an interim measure, he took a one-month position with a busy family practice working 32 hours per week. He agreed to be paid $33 per hour and the employer provided his malpractice insurance. Alex hoped that he could use this time as a working interview, and the job would become permanent at the end of one month.

Throughout the month, Alex and the employer had a couple short discussions about a permanent job. These discussions included the terms of a compensation package and the specifics of Alex's role in the practice. Alex believed he and employer had reached an agreement on the terms, but that his job description itself needed further clarification. At the end of the month, both parties assumed that Alex would continue working, and he did. In fact, Alex worked another two months assuming the permanent agreement was forthcoming.

Toward the end of the third month, Alex decided to write up an employment agreement and job description based on his perception of the discussions he'd had with the employer. Unfortunately, the employer's perception of their discussions was very different from Alex's, and he rejected the agreement. At issue was the salary and incentive. Both had very different ideas as to the previously agreed upon salary. Unable to come to an agreement, Alex's employment ended.

Had the agreement been documented at the time of the early discussions, later discrepancies would have been easily clarified. In all likelihood, Alex would have been gainfully employed.

The following pages contain several ***Sample Agreements*** describing a full time job, a part time job, and one for an independent contractor.** They contain many of the elements discussed in the *Negotiation Planner*.

*Cost of living adjustments can be calculated in several ways. Ask your employer for the basis of his calculations. Merit increases and the way in which they are determined must be spelled out by the employer. It is insufficient to say, "You'll get a raise if you do a good job." When? How much? Your employer may not be able to be as specific as you wish, but try to pin him down as much as possible.

**You must be absolutely certain that if you work as an independent contractor you understand the IRS requirements for doing so. The IRS is very specific about the definition of an independent contractor, and can impose very real consequences for both you and your employer if the requirements are not met. Please seek legal and/or financial advice if you choose to work in this manner.

Full Time *Sample Agreement*
Family Health Center and Emily Waller, PA-C
April 18, 2001

POSITION

Emily Waller ("Practitioner") accepts the employment and responsibilities of Physician Assistant at Family Health Center ("Center"). Practitioner's scope of practice will be limited to primary care and urgent care for low risk patients seen at Center. Nicholas Wheeler, MD, and Marianne Farmer, MD will provide the immediate backup and supervision for the practitioner. Practitioner accepts this position as a 40 hour per week position, and the schedule will be Monday through Friday 9am to 6pm. The schedule is subject to change upon mutual agreement. There will be no call or weekend work.

COMPENSATION

The salary will be $60,320 per year, which is the equivalent of $29 per hour, payable on the second and fourth Friday of each month for the previous period. An increase of $2,080 or $1 per hour will automatically be given at the end of the first 90 days of employment. The salary will be $62,400 for the next nine months. Thereafter, salary increases will be given at a minimum level of 4% per year, and will be given every 12 months, coinciding with the first day of employment.

RETIREMENT

Center agrees to contribute $100 per month toward Practitioner's retirement after the first 12 months of employment. Such contribution will be made directly into an IRA chosen by and maintained by Practitioner. Said IRA must conform to the guidelines set forth by the IRS.

HEALTH INSURANCE

Comprehensive health insurance is available through the Center for Practitioner and his/her dependents after the first 90 days of employment at no cost to Practitioner.

SICK LEAVE

Twelve paid sick days per year are allowed due to illness, and are only to be used for illness. In the event all twelve days are not used, Family Health Center is not obligated to give the Practitioner the balance in time off or dollars.

HOLIDAYS

The following holidays are paid and the office is closed: January 1st, Martin Luther King, Jr. Day, Memorial Day, July 4th, Labor Day, Thanksgiving Day and the day after, Christmas Eve, and Christmas Day.

VACATION

Practitioner is entitled to 10 days per year (2 work weeks) paid time off for vacation in years one and two of employment. Practitioner is eligible to use paid time off for vacation after the first six months of employment. Vacation time will increase to 15 days (3 work weeks) per year after 2 years of employment. After 4 years of employment, vacation time will increase to 16 days (4 work weeks) per year, and will not increase thereafter.

CONTINUING MEDICAL EDUCATION

Center will give five days paid time off to attend CME courses, and pay up to $1,200 toward tuition for CME. No other associated expenses will be reimbursed.

MALPRACTICE INSURANCE

Center will pay for and maintain "Occurrence" malpractice liability insurance for Practitioner in the amount of $1 million per occurrence, and $3 million total claims per year. The carrier is Reliable Insurance Company. Center shall notify Reliable that Practitioner is to be covered by them on the date this agreement commences. This employment agreement is contingent upon the availability of such insurance.

CONTRACTUAL AGREEMENT

The probationary period will be for the first 90 days of employment; during which time either the Practitioner or Center may withdraw from this agreement with one day's notice. Thereafter, both parties agree to give 30 days written notice of such withdrawal. Center can give one month's salary in lieu of one month's written notice to withdraw from this contract.

Performance evaluations will be given at the end of the probationary period and every six months thereafter, or when either party requests one. Salary and benefits will be evaluated every 12 months, and increases will be given on the basis of cost of living adjustment or merit. See "COMPENSATION".

This agreement automatically renews itself on a monthly basis until either party gives one month's notice to terminate employment.

____ Date _________

Emily Waller, PA-C

____ Date _________

Nicholas Wheeler, MD or Marianne Farmer, MD
Family Health Center

Part Time *Sample Agreement*
Family Health Center and Benjamin Harrington, PNP
December 6, 2001

POSITION

Benjamin Harrington("Practitioner") accepts the employment and responsibilities of Pediatric Nurse Practitioner at Family Health Center ("Center"). Practitioner's scope of practice will be limited to the primary care of children and adolescents. Nicholas Wheeler, MD, and Marianne Farmer, MD will provide the immediate backup and supervision for the practitioner. Practitioner accepts this position as a 24 hour per week position, and the schedule will be Tuesday, Wednesday, and Thursday 11am to 8pm. The schedule is subject to change upon mutual agreement. There will be no call or weekend work.

COMPENSATION

Practitioner will be paid $31 per hour, payable on the 15th and 31st of each month for the previous period. An increase of $1.50 per hour will automatically be given at the end of the first six months of employment. In addition, Center will pay Practitioner $5 per patient in excess of 300 patients per month after the first 90 days of employment. Thereafter, base salary increases will be given at a minimum level of 4% per year, and will be given every 12 months, coinciding with the first day of employment. All increases in base salary, bonus, or incentive will be negotiated every 11 months, and any increase will commence with the next month's paycheck.

SICK LEAVE

Seven paid sick days per year are allowed due to illness, and are only to be used for illness. In the event all seven days are not used, Family Health Center is not obligated to reimburse the Practitioner the balance in time off or dollars.

HOLIDAYS

The following holidays are paid and the office is closed: January 1st, Martin Luther King, Jr. Day, Memorial Day, July 4th, Labor Day, Thanksgiving Day and the day after, Christmas Eve, and Christmas Day.

VACATION

Practitioner is entitled to 6 days per year (2 work weeks) paid time off for vacation in years one and two of employment. Practitioner is eligible to use paid time off for vacation after the first six months of employment. Vacation time will increase to 9 days (3 work weeks) per year after 2 years of employment. After 4 years of employment, vacation time will increase to 12 days (4 work weeks) per year, and will not increase thereafter.

CONTINUING EDUCATION

Center will give three days paid time off to attend CE courses, and pay up to $750 toward tuition for CE. No other associated expenses will be reimbursed.

MALPRACTICE INSURANCE

Center will pay for and maintain "Occurrence" malpractice liability insurance for Practitioner in the amount of $1 million per occurrence, and $3 million total claims per year. The carrier is Reliable Insurance Company. Center shall notify Reliable that Practitioner is to be covered by them on the date this agreement commences. This employment agreement is contingent upon the availability of such insurance.

CONTRACTUAL AGREEMENT

The probationary period will be for the first 90 days of employment; during which time either the Practitioner or Center may withdraw from this agreement with one day's notice. Thereafter, both parties agree to give 30 days written notice of such withdrawal. Center can give one month's salary in lieu of one month's written notice to withdraw from this contract.

Performance evaluations will be given at the end of the probationary period and every six months thereafter, or when either party requests one. Salary and benefits will be evaluated every 12 months, and increases will be given on the basis of cost of living adjustment or merit. See "COMPENSATION".

This agreement automatically renews itself on a monthly basis until either party gives one month's notice to terminate employment.

____ Date __________

Benjamin Harrington, PNP

____ Date __________

Nicholas Wheeler, MD or Marianne Farmer, MD
Family Health Center

Independent Contractor *Sample Agreement*
Village Medical Group and Jacob Elliott, PA-C/FNP
September 8, 2001

POSITION

Mr. Jacob Elliott, PA-C/FNP will be responsible for providing primary internal medicine for patients of Village Medical Group. Isabel Zaneda, MD, and Ariana Malin, MD will provide the immediate backup and supervision for the practitioner. Mr. Elliott agrees to work 36 hours per week, and the schedule will be Wednesday, Thursday, and Friday 8am to 8pm. This schedule is subject to change upon mutual agreement.

COMPENSATION

Mr. Elliott will work as an independent contractor and be compensated at the rate of $36 per hour. He will be responsible for submitting billing statements for his services on the 30th and 15th day of each month to Village Medical Group. Mr. Elliott will in turn be paid on the 6th and 21st day of each month. Village Medical Group agrees to provide a summary of compensation in the form of IRS Form 1099 on an annual basis.

VACATION, HOLIDAYS, & SICK LEAVE

Village Medical Group does not provide any paid time off for vacation, holidays, or sick leave. As an independent contractor, Mr. Elliott will notify Village Medical Group of any planned time off at least 30 days in advance, with the exception of unforeseen illness.

MALPRACTICE INSURANCE

Village Medical Group will pay for and maintain "Claims Made" malpractice liability insurance for Mr. Elliott in the amount of $1 million/ $3 million per year. The carrier is Reliable Insurance Company. Village Medical Group shall notify Reliable that Mr. Elliott is to be covered by them on the date this agreement commences. In addition, Mr. Elliott agrees to provide his own additional liability policy of not less than $1 million/$3 million per year that includes tail coverage.

CONTRACTUAL AGREEMENT

This agreement is for a period of 12 months commencing September 8, 2001 and ending September 7, 2002. For the first six months of this agreement, either party can withdraw from this contract without cause with one day's written notice. Thereafter, either party agrees to provide 30 day's advance written notice to withdraw from this agreement. Any changes in the terms of this agreement must be made with mutual consent. This agreement automatically renews itself on an annual basis with the consent of Mr. Jacob Elliott and Village Medical Group.

____ Date _________

Jacob Elliott, PA-C/FNP

____ Date _________

Isabel Zaneda, MD or Ariana Malin, MD
Village Medical Group

PART IV

RESUMES, COVER LETTERS & INTERVIEWING

RESUME PREPARATION
SAMPLE COVER LETTERS
SAMPLE RESUMES
INTERVIEWING

Resumes, Cover Letters & Interviewing

Creating a resume, writing an informative cover letter, and going through the interview process can feel like daunting tasks. They don't have to be. Use the following suggestions to ease your way through.

Resumes

Think about where you've been, what you've done, when you did it, and write it down. That's the backbone of your resume. Use a computer to type your resume and *save it.* Next time you need to add something, the job is simple. It is often thought that a resume in excess of one page is too long. Not true. A two-page resume is common. It is crucial that your resume factually describes your career, and it is often difficult to do yourself justice in less than two pages. However, there is nothing wrong with a one-page resume, as long as it properly describes who you are.

There are as many opinions about resume design, as there are people who write them. Following are two different formats that will give you some ideas. There is nothing written in stone about either one, except their consistency. Please note the use of **bold**, *italics*, <u>underline</u>, and UPPER CASE lettering. Also, the margins are consistent throughout each format. The terms used in the headings for the various categories are arbitrary. If there is a category you need, and it is not mentioned here, add it.

It is important that your resume be easy to read, flowing from one subject to another. Remember to list insertions in reverse chronological order. You want the person reading your resume to immediately know who you are; what you're doing now; what you've done; and what special skills and/or training you have. Resumes of this kind command attention.

A WORD ABOUT OBJECTIVES: Often resumes begin with stated objectives at the top of the page. They typically say, " To obtain a challenging position with a thriving family practice that will utilize my skills and allow personal and professional growth". The person reading your resume already knows that you are looking for a job, and probably has a good idea that a position with growth potential is preferable. Objectives are redundant. Rather, use a carefully worded cover letter outlining your objectives based on your special skills, talents, and availability.

Cover Letters

Factual and succinct cover letters get attention. Keep in mind that long, boastful letters telling the employer why you are the person for the job often end up in the garbage. It is best to err on the side of modesty. Your resume will speak for itself.

As a new graduate, you may feel as though your resume does not speak for itself. In this case, the cover letter is especially important. It's a good idea to describe your experience prior to your training and perhaps why you chose to become a nurse practitioner or physician assistant. Remaining factual and succinct is still a good idea. The following cover letters illustrate the idea.

Interviewing

Most people do not enjoy the interview process, especially when they really need a job. If you already have a job but are looking for a better situation, you have very little to lose and the process is not as difficult. No matter what position you are in, it is best to just be yourself. Employers commonly make judgements about a person in the first minute of an interview, both positive and negative. So the more at ease you are, the more accurate the employer's opinion of you will be and the more accurate your opinion of the job and employer will be as well. Remember, you, too, are interviewing this employer.

In an interview, appearance matters. Be sure you are well groomed, your clothing is clean, pressed and put together. It doesn't need to be fancy, and you don't need to break your budget to purchase just the right outfit, but you must look professional. Do not eat or drink during an interview. Eye contact is very important. Imagine you're having a conversation with a person you really like and it will be easier to be relaxed.

Preparing for the interview is important. While it's impossible to anticipate everything that will be asked of you, it's a good idea to have a few questions of your own prepared. For example:

What is a typical day like in terms of patient volume and kinds of patients?

Do the MD's and NP/PA's meet on a regular basis to review patients?

How long has the practice been in business? Is there more than one office?

Are there any other NP's of PA's in the practice?

Most people are eager to talk about the compensation package in general during the first interview. There is nothing wrong with doing that, but it's a good idea to wait until the end of the meeting to make this inquiry. Be sure you are fairly interested in the job as a whole before getting into the compensation discussion, as it may lead to a lengthy conversation that neither you nor the employer is really ready to have.

At the end of an interview, an employer will usually ask if you have any further questions. If he doesn't ask this question, don't let the interview end without getting a little more information. Be sure to ask when and how you can expect to hear from him. Listen carefully to the answer. It will tell you a lot about this employer's process; whether he is interviewing a number of people, whether or not he has any time constraints to fill this position, and how eager he is to talk with you again. Whether or not there will be further contact, it's a good idea to send the employer a note thanking him for his time and reiterating your interest in the job. The thank you note is another opportunity to make a positive impression.

Sample Cover Letters & Resumes

As you read the following examples, keep in mind your own situation. Use these samples for ideas, but pay particular attention to the consistency in format. Again, there's nothing written in stone. Just be sure that your skills, knowledge and training are clearly illustrated in an easy to follow manner, leaving no question about who you are and what you have to offer.

SAMPLE COVER LETTER – NEW GRADUATE

Julia Isaacs, FNP

1414 Hummingbird Lane, Peachtree, VT 55555, Phone Number

July 10, 2001

William Lawry, MD
678 Street Lane
Emerald, CA 99999

Dear Dr. Lawry:

I am writing to express my interest in seeking a full time position beginning in the fall, as I have just completed my Family Nurse Practitioner training. My experience prior to this training consists of eight years as an RN where my work included both Intensive Care and Emergency Medicine. In addition, I have had extensive experience volunteering in inner city programs for homeless families. My goal is to find a position that will allow me to work with people of all ages, especially those of underserved populations.

For your review, I have enclosed a copy of my resume, references, and current licensure. Thank you very much for your consideration, and I hope to hear from you.

Sincerely,

Julia Isaacs, FNP

Enc.

SAMPLE COVER LETTER

Julia Isaacs, FNP

1414 Hummingbird Lane, Peachtree, VT 55555, Phone Number

May 12, 2001

William Lawry, MD
678 Street Lane
Emerald, CA 99999

Dear Dr. Lawry:

I am writing to express my interest in seeking a full time position beginning in the fall, as my family and I are moving to your community. I am a family nurse practitioner with eight years of experience; five years in internal medicine with special emphasis in geriatrics, and three years in family practice. I am fluent in Spanish, and my goal is to find a position that will allow me to work with Spanish speaking clients.

For your review, I have enclosed a copy of my resume, references, and current licensure. Thank you very much for your consideration, and I hope to hear from you.

Sincerely,

Julia Isaacs, FNP

Enc.

NAME, TITLE
Address, City, State Zip Code, Phone Number, email

EDUCATION

Degree Earned — Year of Completion
Educational Institution
City, State

Degree Earned — Year of Completion
Educational Institution
City, State

CLINICAL SITE EXPERIENCE

Name of Practice, City, State — Date(s)
Provide a short description of your work in this setting.

Name of Practice, City, State — Date(s)
Provide a short description of your work in this setting.

ACADEMIC HONORS

List any — Date

EMPLOYMENT BACKGROUND

Name of Employer, City, State — 1994 to Present
Position held: describe job in several sentences.

Name of Employer, City, State — 1991 to 1994
Position held: describe job in several sentences at the most

LICENSES & CERTIFICATIONS

List all, including license numbers, one insertion per line
ACLS, Current
PALS, Current

VOLUNTEER EXPERIENCE

List all — Dates

Fluent in Spanish (list languages spoken if appropriate)

References Provided Upon Request

NAME, TITLE
Address
City, State Zip Code
Phone Number, email

EDUCATION

Year of Completion	Educational Institution, City, State Degree earned
Year of Completion	Educational Institution, City, State Degree earned

PROFESSIONAL EXPERIENCE

1995 to Present	Name of Employer, City, State *Type of Position (Physician Assistant)*: Description of responsibilities
1992 to 1995	Name of Employer, City, State *Type of Position (Nurse Practitioner)*: Description of responsibilities
etc	etc etc

LICENSES & CERTIFICATIONS

State of ...., Physician Assistant #.............
National Commission for the Certification of Physician Assistants #...........
State of ...., Nurse Practitioner #............
State of ...., Nurse Practitioner Furnishing #..........
etc
etc

MEMBERSHIPS & AFFILIATIONS

State Academy of Physician Assistants
etc

VOLUNTEER EXPERIENCE

List all

Fluent in ....

References Provided Upon Request

Notes

Notes